Art as a Profitable Pursuit

Opening Your Own Gallery or Studio Space

Table of Contents

Chapter 1. Introduction

Unleash the art connoisseur within you as you explore the inspiring realm of our Special Report: "Art as a Profitable Pursuit: Opening Your Own Gallery or Studio Space". This report is filled to the brim with practical insights and strategies to transform your passion for art into a successful entrepreneurship journey. We'll walk you through the diverse world of art, helping you outline the necessary steps for setting up your own gallery or studio. Along the way, you'll discover how art is not just a medium of expression but also a ripe, flourishing industry worth investing your time and resources. Whether you're an artist yearning to share your work with a wider audience or an art enthusiast dreaming of curating your own collection, this special report will get your dreams off the ground. So, ready to mingle your creative passion with a flair for business? Get your hands on this exclusive guide today and start plotting your path in the artistic landscape!

Chapter 2. Laying the Foundation: Understanding the Art Market

Delving into the enchanting world of art entrepreneurship begins with a comprehensive understanding of the art market. The art market is the marketplace or public plaza where art is bought and sold, and it offers a wealth of opportunities for artists and gallery owners.

2.1. Decoding the Art Market

The art market can be cryptic to the uninitiated. Once you peel away the layers, however, it revolves around two major areas: the primary market and the secondary market.

In the primary market, new works of art are sold for the first time. This typically involves direct transactions between artists and collectors, or via intermediaries such as galleries or agents. The price in the primary market is usually set by the artist or their representative.

In contrast, the secondary market consists of works that have been sold at least once before. Auction houses, dealers, and galleries are the primary drivers of the secondary market. The price here is determined by demand, historical significance, condition, and provenance.

2.2. Fluctuations in Market Trends

Understanding the behaviour of the art market requires a close watch on trends and their fluctuations. The art world, like other sectors, is subject to economic ups and downs, societal changes, and shifts in aesthetic preference. Trends can vary wildly from year to year, with different genres or styles of art falling in and out of favour.

Keeping a finger on the pulse of these trends will help you anticipate which artworks are likely to gain value and popularity. Subscribing to art publications, attending art fairs, and establishing networks with artists and other gallery owners are effective ways of staying informed.

2.3. Understanding Art Valuation

Art valuation is a critical aspect of the art market that heavily influences buying and selling decisions. Several components play into the valuation of an artwork, including:

1. Artist's reputation: A well-established or well-known artist's work usually commands a higher price.

2. Rarity: Rare works, or works from an artist's limited period or series, can increase in value.

3. Condition: Works in excellent condition are usually more valuable.

4. Provenance: A well-documented history of ownership can enhance a piece's value.

5. Market trends: As mentioned earlier, current market trends greatly affect an artwork's worth.

While it is crucial to consider these factors, remember that art is subjective, and its value can often be tied to individual preference and perception.

2.4. The Role of Auction Houses

Auction houses play a significant role in the secondary art market. They bring reputable artworks to the market, pulling in a plethora of interested buyers. Some of the major auction houses, like Sotheby's, Christie's, and Bonhams, not only sell works but also provide valuation services. They can help determine market demand and set a realistic estimate for specific pieces of art.

2.5. The Significance of Art Fairs

Art fairs are momentous events in the art world calendar and are crucial hubs for the art market. Not only do these events allow artists and galleries to network and sell work, but they also give buyers a chance to discover new artists and browse a vast array of pieces from different genres and periods.

Attending art fairs gives you invaluable exposure to the current market dynamics, upcoming trends, as well as procurement and networking opportunities.

2.6. Building Your Network

In the art market, building a strong network can be invaluable. This network can include other art dealers, collectors, artists, curators, critics, and industry influencers. In addition to enriching your understanding of the market, a solid network can help access new art pieces, get insider information about emerging artists, and offer opportunities for collaboration.

2.7. Investing in the Art Market

While art can undoubtedly be a lucrative investment, it's essential to approach it thoughtfully. Several pieces of advice for investing in the art market would include, doing comprehensive research before investing, diversifying your art portfolio, and always being passionate about the pieces you invest in. After all, while profitability is significant, the real joy of participating in the art market often comes from the sheer love for art itself.

In conclusion, understanding the art market involves getting to grips with market dynamics, valuation principles, significant players, and investing wisely. By understanding these elements, you are better equipped to navigate the intriguing journey of opening your own gallery or studio successfully.

Chapter 3. Unleashing the Entrepreneur: Your Role in the Art World

Artistic entrepreneurship requires a fine balance—connecting artistic creativity with the nuances of business and management. Your role as an entrepreneur in the world of art is one filled with opportunities and challenges. Ensuring you're well-equipped to navigate this role requires understanding its facets, from marketing your unique artistic products to fostering relationships in the art community, and developing strategies that spotlight creativity while yielding financial success.

3.1. Understanding Your Role

As an entrepreneur in the art world, you will wear many hats. You'll be the executive director, curator, marketer, salesperson, perhaps juggling all at once. This can be daunting for those used to focusing solely on the artistic aspect but understanding the scope of your role is crucial to succeed.

Your primary function will be to manage your business, which means ensuring you balance your books and generate enough income to sustain and grow. Alongside, you'll need a curatorial eye, choosing the art you want to promote or sell in your gallery or studio space. Marketing and sales will also fall under your purview, requiring you to function as a public relations representative and communicate with potential buyers. Simultaneously, you would need to manage staff, establish and maintain relationships within the art community, and above all, stay passionate and informed about the art you showcase.

3.2. Creating Synergy: Art and Business

Art is emotion and business is logic. In truth, your role will be merging these two realms. While it may seem these spheres clash, they can harmoniously co-exist - art brings uniqueness and emotional connection, attracting customers, and sound business strategies ensure sustainability and growth. The harmony between these realms is your golden ticket.

Understanding and appreciating your product establishes your authenticity as an artistic entrepreneur. This passion will help you sell your products more effectively. On the other hand, understanding the value of money, setting up appropriate price points, forecasting sales, and drafting a business plan are as vital.

3.3. Prepare With Knowledge

Arming yourself with knowledge — of art, business, and the intricate web that connects the two — is essential. Comprehensive understanding of art history, current trends, and future predictions help to visualize and adopt suitable business models. Networking and forming connections within the art community aids in acquiring unique pieces and staying updated with the industry's pulse.

Enhancing your business knowledge, particularly about starting a new business, managing finances, creating marketing campaigns, and understanding the digital world is key. In today's world, a good entrepreneur must know how to leverage digital channels to promote their brand and products.

3.4. Ethics and Authenticity in Art

Promoting truth and authenticity in your venture is pivotal for its long-term success. As a gallery owner or studio operator, the art you choose to showcase will reflect your vision and authenticity. Display work that resonates with your beliefs, pushing forward original creators' work and avoiding copies or forgeries.

Adhering to ethical business practices is paramount. Ensuring fair pricing, acknowledging artists' rights, promoting inclusivity, and following legal norms can solidify your reputation as a trustworthy entrepreneur.

3.5. Building A Sustainable Business Model

As an entrepreneur, your success largely depends on the business model you choose. Studios and galleries operate on different models; whether you charge a commission, run on membership, or employ a different strategy entirely will greatly affect your viability.

Consider the high initial costs. Investing in a physical space, renovation, initial inventory, and getting started can be quite high. Develop a plan for these initial investments and your ongoing operating costs, such as utilities, salaries, insurance, and maintenance.

Running a successful art-based business means keeping your finger on the pulse of the art world. Regularly attend art shows, participate in fairs and network with artists and fellow gallery owners to stay current. Always keep searching for the new and interesting, as this industry thrives on standing out from the crowd.

3.6. Diving into the Digital World

The power of the digital age cannot be overstated. Developing a robust online presence heightens visibility, extends your market beyond geographical boundaries, and gives a boost to sales. An aesthetically designed website with high-resolution images of your collection, artist descriptions, price information, and online purchasing options can draw potential buyers from around the globe.

Social media platforms offer unprecedented opportunities for direct engagement with customers and artists. Regular updates showcasing new additions, providing behind-the-scenes looks, and weaving stories around displayed pieces can mesmerize your audience and build loyalty.

3.7. Conclusion

Being an entrepreneur in the art world bridges creative expression and business acumen. The joy of sharing compelling artwork with the public blends with the rewarding challenge of running a successful business. With sufficient dedication, knowledge, and resourcefulness, you have the potential to transform the lives of artists and art enthusiasts alike, all while fulfilling your entrepreneurial aspirations. Now that you have an outline of your role and the steps it includes, the small, everyday decisions towards this ambitious goal will weave the path to your success. The world of art awaits your unique touch.

Chapter 4. The Business Canvas: Creating a Solid Business Plan

Creating a well-thought-out business plan for your art gallery or studio space is not a buzzkill to your creative vibe but rather a ground-breaking tool to materialize your entrepreneurial dreams. It provides you with a game plan, guiding you on the tactical path while visualizing your strategic approach in the art industry. An art business, just like any other business, needs a solid blueprint outlining the structure of your operations, your objectives, and the strategies you'll adopt to achieve these goals.

4.1. Understanding Your Business Model

A business model is more than just how you make money; it's your business's foundation – determining how you operate, generate sales, and produce profits to power your entrepreneurial journey. Begin by establishing your value proposition, which is the unique value of your goods or services. As an art gallery or studio owner, your value proposition could be providing an exclusive collection of art, offering spaces for artists to create their artwork, or even hosting art workshops.

You should also consider how you will establish customer relationships. Will you network at art events? Will you partner with local artists or art schools? Specify your channels of distribution too. Will you primarily sell or showcase work in a physical location or incorporate online sales, particularly in this digital age? Detail these aspects in your business model.

4.2. Market Research

Effective art market research is about understanding your potential customers, their preferences, and market trends. Subsequently, you harness this information to meet and exceed customer expectations. You can conduct market research by exploring social media platforms, observing competitor activities, attending art fairs, or simply, conversing with artists and art collectors.

4.3. Competitor Analysis

A detailed competitor analysis allows you to identify your competitors' strengths and weaknesses, providing you with insights on gaps you can fill in the market. Study your competitors' business models, look at their pricing strategies, and examine their marketing strategies to get ahead of the curve.

4.4. Marketing and Sales Strategy

Promotion is a critical success factor in the art industry. Design a marketing plan that will grab attention—leverage social media, art blogs, local newspapers, and anything that gets your gallery or studio in the public eye. Organize local art fairs or collaborate with other local businesses to create art events. It's important also your pricing strategy matches the value you're providing without deterring potential buyers.

4.5. Organizational Structure and Management Team

An efficient gallery or studio requires an effective team. Detail your organizational structure—list your staff roles, responsibilities, and necessary skills. Even if you are starting alone, speculating on potential roles can shed light on areas where you may want or need help in the future.

4.6. Financial Projections

In this section, outline your financial projections and profitability estimates. This includes your revenue streams, break-even analysis, sales forecasts, and expense budget. If you're seeking investors or a loan, you'll need to provide financial statements and a balance sheet as well.

4.7. Risk Assessment

Starting a business comes with risk. Identifying these potential pitfalls in advance helps you devise strategies to mitigate them. Risks could be anything from financial uncertainties to changes in the art market.

4.8. Conclusion

A sturdy business plan is the bedrock of your successful entrepreneurship journey in the art industry. It helps you stay organized, plan for the future, and refine your business idea. More importantly, a business plan can help you secure an investor if needed. Take time to work on this strategic document for it has the power to turn your dreams into reality.

As each art business is unique, so will be each business plan. Remember to keep your business plan living, flexible to changes as you grow, and reflective of your visions and ambitions in the art industry. The artistic world awaits your marvelous contributions!

Chapter 5. Securing the Keys: Finding the Perfect Space

Securing an appropriate location is crucial when planning to open up your own gallery or studio. It's not just about finding a place large enough to exhibit the works of art, but it's also about finding a location that will attract a certain type of clientele and provide a unique, immersive experience. Elements such as geographical location, neighborhood character, building architecture, and rental cost can significantly affect your gallery or studio's success.

5.1. Evaluate Your Needs

Before embarking on the search for the perfect location, conduct a thorough analysis of your needs and requirements. How much space do you need to exhibit the artworks? Do you require additional storage or back-office rooms? Do you want a ground floor or garden space for outdoor installations or sculptures? Is there a need for private viewing rooms or workshops? Assessing these needs will help you decide on your property parameters and narrow down your search.

5.2. Set a Budget

Setting a realistic budget from the outset is important. This not only includes the rental or purchasing costs but also the operational expenses such as maintenance, utilities, and insurance. Remember, size and location will significantly influence the cost. Consider hiring a real estate professional to guide you through the financial aspects and help you negotiate the best deal.

Remember that setting a budget and sticking to it is essential in the initial stages. Going over-budget in securing a space could hurt your business in the long-run if you're then unable to sustain other key business functions.

5.3. Scope the Market

Once you have a clear understanding of your needs and budget, scout the market for potential locations. You could use online platforms, engage property agents or even network with other gallery or studio owners for leads.

When scouting the market, ensure you consider the following three main aspects:

1. Accessibility and Visibility: The location should be easily accessible for your target audience, preferably in an area with high foot traffic. Frontage visibility is also a significant factor in drawing spontaneous visitors.

2. Locality: The neighborhood should ideally support the arts and attract a likeminded population. If your target audience are the affluent, consider upscale neighborhoods, whereas a younger, hipper audience might be attracted to an artsy, urban locale.

3. Size and Layout: The size should accommodate your operations with a layout that allows visitors to move around easily. High ceilings, good lighting, and wall space are important for an art gallery.

5.4. Visit Potential Locations

Next, make appointments to physically inspect potential sites. Carry a checklist of your requirements and questions to ask the property owner or agent. Note the condition of the space, the visibility, parking facilities, and proximity to public transportation, among others.

During visits, take photographs and notes which can be reviewed later for decision-making. Sometimes, you might also get an instinctive feel of the space, whether it matches your vision for the gallery or studio.

5.5. Negotiate Agreement Terms and Sign a Lease

Once you've zeroed in on a suitable location, prepare to negotiate. It's best to involve a legal expert to ensure you understand the terms of the lease or sale agreement. You want to avoid any hidden costs or restrictions that might affect your business operations. Once you're comfortable with the agreed terms, sign the agreement.

Securing the keys to your dream gallery or studio is just the beginning. The perfect space sets the foundation, but the success of your venture lies in how you leverage this space to present beautiful art and provide visitors an exemplary experience.

Remember, the perfect location is one that aligns with your vision while meeting practical considerations chicly and affordably. Once the location is finalized, you're on your way to transforming this space into a thriving landscape of creativity and commerce.

Chapter 6. The Art of Curation: Selecting Artists and Works to Showcase

First and foremost, as a to-be gallerist or studio owner, it's critical that you embrace the role of a curator. This role requires a delicately balanced blend of meticulous planning, profound understanding of the art landscape, intuition, and respect for artistic creativity.

6.1. Understanding The Broad Spectrum Of Art

Understanding the artistic landscape is a crucial first step towards successful curation. This means acknowledging and appreciating the diversity of styles, themes, mediums, and techniques, as well as the flux of trends within the art world. This knowledge provides a solid foundation for selecting the artists and works you wish to showcase.

Spend time visiting museums, galleries, and artists' studios, and attend art fairs and auctions. Submerge yourself into art literature such as journals, catalogues, and books to augment your understanding. Also, stay updated with art-related conversations on social media platforms and art forums. This will enhance your comprehension of current popular themes, emerging artists, and new techniques being leveraged.

Embrace variety in your exploration and consider multiple dimensions of art – from contemporary to classic, digital to traditional, minimalistic to ornate, and everything in between – to build a comprehensive understanding.

6.2. Selecting Artists

Choosing the right artists to work with is a critical aspect of your curation strategy. You need to consider not just the quality of an artist's work, but also their ethos, vision, and potential longevity in the market.

Here's a practical guide to your artist selection:

1. List your preferred artists with their corresponding body of works.

2. Take time to study each artist's journey, motivation, techniques, and idiosyncrasies.

3. Identify the artists who resonate with your gallery's vision and philosophy.

4. Evaluate each artist's market standing and future potential. This includes assessing their previous exhibits, sales history, clientele, and industry reputation.

5. Consider the artist's willingness and ability to collaborate. This includes their openness to feedback, flexibility in case of changes, and professionalism in handling business.

6. Finally, trust your intuition. Often, your subconscious can help pinpoint the right fit.

6.3. Selecting Artworks

Once you've identified your pool of artists, the next task at hand would be selecting pieces to display. While artistic appreciation is subjective, a few factors can guide your decision-making process:

1. Relevancy of themes - You should select pieces that fit within the overall thematic guidelines of your gallery or studio.

2. Aesthetic Consistency - While variety is necessary to cater to

diverse tastes, ensuring coherence among the displayed pieces enhances overall appeal.

3. Market trends - While not being governed solely by trends, being aware of what sells can help attract more visitors.

4. Originality - Exciting, innovative pieces can command attention and make your gallery stand out.

5. Condition - The condition of the artwork can significantly affect its market value and appeal to clients.

6.4. Building Relationships

Building a strong relationship with the artists you decide to work with is fundamental to your gallery or studio's success. Engage with them regularly, show interest in their work and respect their creative processes. This mutual respect and understanding can foster a productive and lasting partnership.

6.5. Frequent Review and Adaptation

The art world, like any other industry, is dynamic and shifting. Keep reviewing your selection strategy, update it with changing trends, and learn from experiences and feedback.

Running a gallery or studio is, in many ways, akin to the complexities of curating - it requires an understanding of the art world, a deep appreciation for creative expression, and a firm grasp of business dynamics. However, with commitment, passion and a well-planned strategy, it's perfectly possible to turn your gallery or studio into an uplifting space of artistic celebration and a lucrative enterprise.

Chapter 7. Building Relationships: Networking in the Art Community

Engaging with the art community is integral to establishing a successful gallery or studio. It provides you with several opportunities for learning, collaboration, and growth. Yet, many people find networking to be a daunting task. Fear not, though, as there are numerous ways to navigate the art community with ease and confidence.

7.1. Defining Your Goals

Before embarking upon any networking journey, it is crucial to define your goals clearly. What are you hoping to achieve from these relationships? Are you aiming to collaborate, learn, spread awareness about your gallery or studio, or all of the above? Having clear objectives will help guide your networking efforts in the right direction.

Let's acknowledge the fact that networking isn't simply about amassing contacts. It's about building mutually beneficial relationships. Understand what you want, but also be aware of what you can offer in return. Be it insights, collaborative projects, or a fresh perspective, having something to offer makes you a valuable asset in any network.

7.2. Understanding the Art Community Landscape

The art community is a rich tapestry of individuals with diverse skillsets, motivations, and outlooks. It extends beyond artists and also includes curators, critics, collectors, and educators. Research and learn about different community members, their roles, and how they could potentially intersect with your interests, and align with your goals. Understanding this landscape will help you strategize your networking efforts effectively.

7.3. Approaching Artists and Their Work

Artists often form the cornerstone of the art community. Approaching artists for collaborations, exhibitions, or talks can be an excellent way to foster strong, symbiotic relationships.

When dealing with artists, show genuine interest in their work. Understand their inspirations, motivations, and techniques. Develop an informed perspective on their art before initiating conversations.

7.4. Networking Events and Opportunities

Networking is, at heart, about connecting with people, and what better way to do this than at social events dedicated to the cause. Art fairs, exhibitions, open studios, auctions, and seminars make for perfect occasions to engage with different individuals from the art community. Attend these events regularly, exchanging ideas, sharing your vision, and making connections.

Moreover, be prepared to seize spontaneous networking opportunities that may present themselves in everyday situations. An open mind and a readiness to engage often pave the pathway to the most rewarding and unexpected connections.

7.5. Developing Relationship-building Strategies

A successful networking strategy contains multiple elements, ranging from communication skills to follow-up techniques. Start by honing your elevator pitch, a concise and engaging description of who you are, what you do, and what you aim to achieve.

Following up after making a contact is equally important in building robust relationships. A simple email or social media message can reinforce the connection. From time to time, share useful information, articles, or opportunities that your contacts may find interesting or beneficial.

Lastly, patience is a virtue in networking. Building meaningful relationships takes time—it's a marathon, not a sprint.

7.6. Digital Networking: Leveraging Social Media Platforms

In a world increasingly dominated by digital interaction, leveraging social media platforms like Instagram, LinkedIn, Twitter, and Facebook for networking is a must. Apart from creating and uploading compelling content about your gallery or studio, actively engaging in online communities can help grow your network.

Start by following art influencers, sharing, commenting on their posts, and meaningfully engaging with their content. Take part in groups and forums dedicated to art, contribute to ongoing discussions, ask questions, and share your insights.

7.7. Nurturing and Maintaining Relationships

Networking doesn't end when you've made a useful contact; maintaining and nurturing the relationship is just as important. Show genuine interest in others' work, offer help when possible, share resources, and celebrate their achievements. Developing an attitude of giving before receiving ensures your relationships are meaningful and long-lasting.

In summary, networking in the art community can be a fulfilling endeavor that paves the way for professional growth. Remember, it's not just about creating business opportunities but also about fostering a community of learning, sharing, and collaboration. Start locally, then expand your horizons, engage genuinely, and steadily build your art community network.

Chapter 8. Marketing Masterpiece: Promoting Your Gallery or Studio

An efficient marketing approach can make the difference between a thriving art gallery attracting budding artists and enthusiastic art lovers, and a studio that remains unseen. In this modern age, offering high-quality, well-curated artwork is not enough. You need to effectively promote your business, connect with your target audience, and create momentum in the marketplace.

8.1. Crafting Your Unique Brand Identity

Your brand identity is the essence of your gallery or studio. It's not just about how you present your business, but more importantly, how your audience perceives you. Your brand identity should reflect the evocative nature of the artwork you showcase and the unique business values you hold dear.

First, you need to develop a brand strategy outlining your mission, vision, and objectives. These aspects will shape your brand, making it unique and utterly yours.

Additionally, a compelling and distinctive logo that reflects your gallery's personality, and a catchy tagline that summarizes the essence of your brand, can significantly help in establishing brand recall.

Remember, consistency is key for effective brand identity. From your website and social media accounts to your print materials and in-house decorations, it's crucial to ensure your brand is clearly and consistently represented.

8.2. Building an Engaging Website

In the digital era, having a professional, well-structured website is imperative. Your website is your business' digital home. It acts as the primary channel for showcasing your artwork, sharing artists' stories, and promoting upcoming exhibitions or events.

Your aim should be to create a visually appealing and functional online gallery where visitors can browse artwork, learn about featured artists, and stay updated with gallery events. Implement high-resolution images, intuitive navigation, and descriptive text to invite interaction and keep visitors engaged.

Ensure your website integrates smoothly with e-commerce platforms if you plan to sell artworks online. Payment gateways, shopping cart functionalities, and strong security features are all essential components for a successful e-commerce platform.

Consider the SEO-optimized content, including image tags and descriptions, to enhance your site's visibility on search engines.

8.3. Harnessing the Power of Social Media

Leverage the power of social media to reach a wider audience, engage with them, and build a loyal following. Each social media platform provides a unique way to share content and interact with your followers.

Instagram, with its visual focus and engaged user base, is ideal for showcasing artwork. Use captivating captions that tell the artwork's backstory and employ relevant hashtags to expand reach.

Facebook, on the other hand, is excellent for sharing event updates, blog posts, and conducting live Q&A sessions. Facebook's targeted ads also offer a powerful tool for reaching potential customers based on demographics and interests.

LinkedIn is great for professional networking and connecting with artists, suppliers, and potential partners, while Twitter is perfect for quick updates, sharing industry news, and participating in real-time conversations.

8.4. PR and Media Outreach

Engaging with the media and PR is crucial to getting your gallery or studio noticed. Reach out to local newspapers, art magazines, and bloggers. Share interesting press releases about upcoming exhibitions or new artist signings.

Offer unique story angles to attract journalists and make their job easier. For instance, the inspiring story of an artist you represent, how your gallery is contributing to the local art scene, or the impact of your gallery on community development can be compelling narratives.

8.5. Email Marketing

Despite the rise of social media, email remains a powerful marketing tool. It allows you to directly reach people who have expressed interest in your gallery or studio. You can share regular updates, exhibition invites, or artist features.

To maximize the potential of email marketing, focus on creating meaningful content that adds value to your subscribers. Personalize the experience as much as possible. Segmentation based on subscribers' preferences can go a long way in delivering content that resonates.

8.6. Networking and Partnerships

Creating solid relationships within the art community can reap significant benefits. Attend art fairs, exhibitions, and industry events to network with artists, curators, critics, and potential clients.

Form strategic partnerships. Collaborating with local businesses, artists, and non-profit organizations can provide mutual benefits, including increased visibility and credibility.

8.7. Evaluating and Adjusting Your Marketing Strategy

Lastly, remember the importance of evaluating your marketing strategies regularly. Metrics including website traffic, social media engagement, and email open rates provide invaluable data to adjust and optimize your approach.

Every gallery or studio is unique. What works well for one may not work for another. Be flexible and dynamic in your approach, learn from experience, and don't be afraid to try new things.

Remember, promoting your gallery or studio is not an overnight task. It takes time to build a strong brand, grow your audience, and cultivate loyal relationships. However, with a clear vision, a strong commitment, and a touch of creativity, you can effectively market your art gallery or studio, creating a business that is not only profitable but also contributes positively to the world of art.

Chapter 9. Sustainable Success: Turning a Profit and Maintaining Cash Flow

Running an art gallery or a studio takes more than just passion for the craft – it's a business where profits need to be made and cash flow must be maintained. Taking care of the practicalities does not make you any less of an artist. Instead, it allows you to pursue your art full-time and potentially even become a lifeline for other artists trying to establish themselves in the industry.

9.1. The Art of Making Money

In any business endeavor, understanding the potential revenue sources is paramount. As the owner of an art gallery or studio space, you have opportunities to:

1. Sell Artwork: This is the most obvious revenue stream for an art gallery. How you source the artwork, whether from established artists, emerging talent, or your own work, will largely determine your sales.

2. Run Art Exhibitions: These can be excellent drivers for revenue. Not only might they lead to the sale of artwork, but they can also generate ticket revenues and curated event charges. The cachet of high-profile or unique events can also increase the reputation and visibility of your gallery.

3. Offer Art Classes: If your space allows, providing art classes can attract a continuous customer base and regular income.

4. Rent out the Space: You can rent out your gallery or studio space for various functions and events.

Knowing the ways money can come in will help you make key

decisions for your business. For example, if you're specializing in high-investment pieces, you might focus on sales and exclusive exhibitions. However, if you're running a community-oriented gallery, art classes and space rentals might represent larger income streams.

9.2. Mastering the Art of Money Management

To maintain sustainability, you must manage your earnings as effectively as possible. The following aspects need your attention:

1. Budgeting: One of the first steps when planning for sustainability is creating a detailed and realistic budget. This budget should contain all your projected income streams and expenses, detailed to the smallest level possible. This plan will allow you to ensure your proposed business model can genuinely turn a profit.

2. Regular Financial Review: In addition to a solid initial budget, regular financial reviews are essential to maintaining cash flow. These reviews will help identify any potential shortfalls while also highlighting areas where revenue is higher than expected.

3. Cost Management: A significant part of remaining cash positive is controlling your costs. This practice may include negotiating better deals with suppliers, evaluating staffing needs, or seeking lower-cost methods to market your gallery.

4. Pricing: Pricing your products and services correctly is crucial. Pricing is a delicate balance: you have to consider the perceived value of the artwork, the market rates, and your operating costs.

9.3. The Importance of a Rainy Day Fund

Operating any business carries a certain level of risk, and it is prudent to be prepared for potential downturns. Building a financial buffer, often referred to as a 'rainy day fund,' is an essential financial strategy. This fund can act as an insurance policy if unforeseen expenses arise or if cash inflow temporarily ceases.

9.4. The Role of Good Relationships

A thriving art gallery or studio isn't about figures on a balance sheet. It's about relationships. Fostering meaningful partnerships with artists, customers, suppliers, and the community can lead to greater success. Good relationships can also be a safety net during challenging times, providing moral support and potentially financial assistance.

To succeed in the world of art galleries and studios, it is necessary to combine an aesthetic vision with a keen business sense. Sustainable success isn't about chasing profits at all costs – it's about building a business model that allows your gallery to prosper while contributing to the artistic community.

Chapter 10. Legal Considerations: Licensing and Regulations

Before you can even begin to think about forging relationships with artists and customers, decorating your gallery space, or even opening your doors, there are numerous legal considerations to address. These can seem daunting, but viewed as a whole, they represent a diligent approach to creating the foundation for a successful gallery or studio venture.

Navigating the realm of legalities involves a multitude of tasks, and while this might seem overwhelming, we've broken down this chapter into several sections intending to make it as accessible as possible.

10.1. Obtaining Necessary Licenses

Firstly, and most importantly, you need to secure the proper licenses and permits. While requirements vary from place to place, you will likely need to obtain a general business license at a minimum. Some cities may require additional permits specific to art galleries or studios, so it's crucial to research local regulations and adhere to them strictly. Contact your local government or consult a legal advisor to ensure you're legally compliant and not facing potential penalties.

10.2. Understanding Zoning Laws

Secondly, you may be required to conform to local zoning laws. These laws determine the type of business that can operate in a specific area. For example, some areas may be zoned for residential use only, meaning you'll need to seek an area that allows commercial use if you wish to open your gallery or studio there.

10.3. Complying with ADA Regulations

If your gallery or studio will be open to the public, it's also essential to consider the Americans with Disabilities Act (ADA). Under ADA requirements, you'll need to ensure that your location is accessible to people with disabilities. This could involve providing ramps for wheelchairs, signage for the hearing impaired, or other necessary accommodations.

10.4. Labor and Employment Laws

Should you choose to hire employees, you'll need to familiarize yourself with labor and employment laws. These laws cover a vast range of subjects, from minimum wage requirements and overtime pay to work safety regulations and anti-discrimination laws. Failure to comply with these requirements can result in substantial penalties and legal issues.

10.5. Intellectual Property Laws

Crucial to the art world are the laws surrounding intellectual property. These laws exist to protect artists' rights to their own work. As a gallery or studio owner, you'll be tangled with these on a regular basis. Copyright, the right given to an artist to reproduce their work, is of particular interest. You'll need to ensure that any work you display or sell in your gallery has the required permissions from the artist.

10.6. Sales Tax and VAT

Consideration should also be taken regarding sales tax and value added tax (VAT). Depending on your location, you could be required to collect these taxes on any art sold in your gallery and remit them to the government. It's important to set up a system for tracking these sales and taxes from the get-go to avoid any potential complications down the line.

10.7. Health and Safety Regulations

Moreover, you must be aware of health and safety regulations, particularly if your studio involves the use of potentially hazardous materials. Regulations may dictate whether or not you can store certain materials on-site, require specific ventilation or waste disposal systems, or enforce other rules specific to the nature of your business.

From obtaining licenses to understanding and complying with an array of regulations, opening your own gallery or studio space can be an intricate process. However, by doing your due diligence and seeking expert advice when necessary, you can ensure that your venture is built on a solid legal foundation, setting the stage for success. Understanding these intricacies paves the way for you to focus on the creative and engaging part of the art business which is, after all, the heart and soul of your venture.

Chapter 11. Looking Ahead: Future Trends in the Art Industry

The art industry continually evolves, influenced by myriad societal, technology, and market forces. To plan ahead for a successful gallery or studio, understanding these trends before they become mainstream is crucial.

11.1. Digitization and the Online Art Market

In a study by Hiscox Art Trade Report, online art sales amassed up to $4.82 billion in 2018, a 72% increase from five years earlier. The proliferating trend of digitization has made art more accessible, extending its reach to potential buyers who might not typically walk into an old-school gallery or studio.

With social media platforms like Instagram and Facebook, artists now have the opportunity to showcase their works to a broader audience. There are also numerous e-commerce platforms such as Etsy and Artsy that facilitate online art transactions. For new gallery owners or studio owners, creating an online presence alongside the physical space can lead to larger sales, more social interactions, and extended geographical reach.

Blockchain, the technology underlying cryptocurrencies such as Bitcoin, is another budding trend in online art trade. As the art world suffers from problems of forgery and lack of transparency in pricing, blockchain's decentralized nature can help establish provenance and facilitate a fair price for artworks.

11.2. Rise of Experiential Art

Art has vastly converted from being an object-oriented experience to an immersive one. This can drastically influence the kind of art you choose to display in your gallery or create in your studio.

Art exhibitions such as Yayoi Kusama's Infinity Mirrored Rooms and teamLab's Borderless Museum in Japan have captivated audiences with their immersive installations. These experiences go beyond passive viewing to actively engaging the viewers. Such is the popularity of these installations that they have transformed into 'Art-tainment', a commercially viable enterprise blurring the lines between art, entertainment, and retail.

11.3. Shift to Sustainable Art Practices

The trending concern for environmental damage has substantially influenced art practices. Artists are addressing issues like climate change, pollution, and waste through their artwork, while consciously adopting sustainable art practices.

Materials used for creating art exhibits, including oil paints, acrylics, varnishes, and other toxins, have a detrimental environmental impact. Increasingly, artists are adopting ecologically friendly materials. For gallery or studio owners, showing such conscious artists can attract a more environmentally conscious consumer base.

11.4. Emerging Markets in the Global Art Scene

The epicenter of the art market is shifting with the rise of new players. While traditionally led by the United States and Europe, emerging markets such as China, the Middle East, and Latin America are attaining prominence in the global art scene.

The Chinese art market's growth, in particular, has been meteoric. In 2017, it accounted for 21% of the total global art sales. This shift is essential for gallery and studio owners to note and adapt to the tastes and sensibilities of these markets.

11.5. The Significance of Art Fairs

Art fairs have become a pivotal part of the art industry, influencing trends and dictating the pace of art sales. Gaining popularity for their convenience, these multi-day events showcase a plethora of artists and galleries under one roof, pulling in crowds of artists, collectors, and enthusiasts.

With major fairs like Art Basel and The Armory Show, buyers get to see an overview of what is trending in the art world. For gallery and studio owners, participation in art fairs can lead to extensive networking, audience reach, and potential sales.

11.6. The Substantial Role of Art Advisors

Art advisors play an influential role in linking artists and collectors. Their expertise is sought after by collectors looking for investment pieces, art selection, and negotiation on their behalf. As these advisors often work in establishing upcoming artists, collaboration with them can boost the growth of your gallery or studio.

Despite the increasing complexity and rapid changes in the art industry, it continues to be a dynamic and promising sector to venture into. Its future will be shaped by ongoing trends, technological advances, and socio-political shifts, warranting continuous learning and adaptability. As an aspiring gallery owner or studio owner, understanding these trends will help navigate this multilayered landscape and ensure a fruitful journey in the fascinating world of art.